Time for Tea!

with Mary Engelbreit

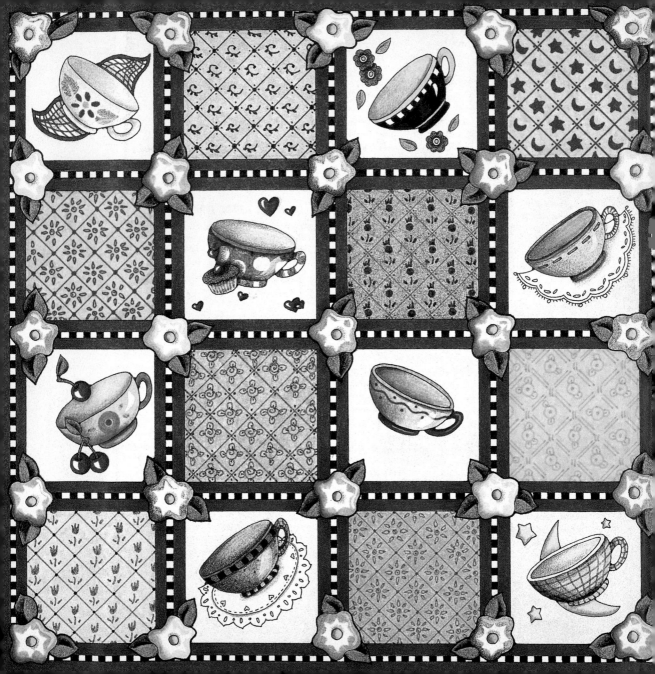

a book about tea

Time for Tea!
with Mary Engelbreit

Illustrated by Mary Engelbreit

Photography by Barbara Elliott Martin

**Andrews McMeel
Publishing**

Kansas City

is a registered trademark of Mary Engelbreit Enterprises, Inc.

Library of Congress Cataloging-in-Publication Data

Engelbreit, Mary.
   Time for tea with Mary Engelbreit / illustrated by Mary Engelbreit ; photography by Barbara Elliott Martin.
     p.   cm.
   ISBN 0-8362-2770-0
   1. Afternoon teas.   2. Tea.   I. Title.
TX736.E54   1997
641.5'3--dc21   96-52595
                                             CIP

Design by Stephanie Raaf

ATTENTION: SCHOOLS AND BUSINESSES

Andrews McMeel books are available at quantity discounts with bulk purchase for educational, business, or sales promotional use. For information, please write to: Special Sales Department, Andrews McMeel Publishing, 4520 Main Street, Kansas City, Missouri 64111.

For
Alice
Queen of the Mothers
·In·Law

contents

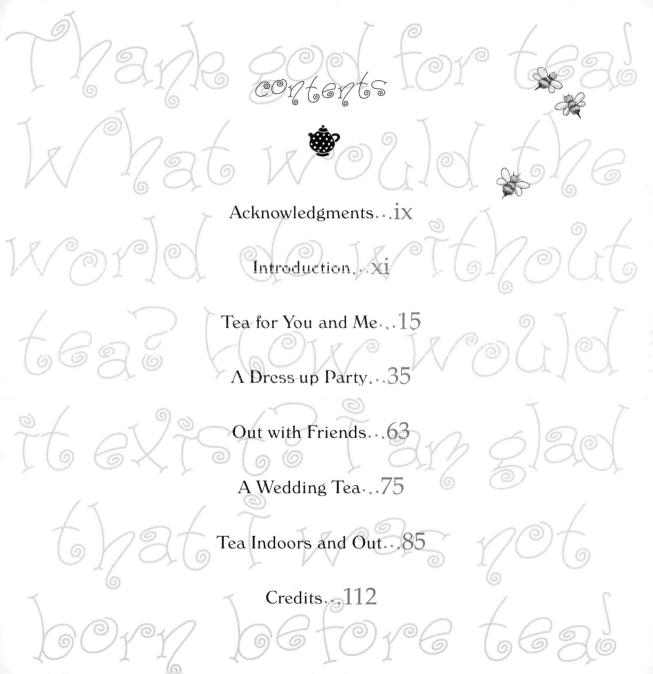

grateful appreciation to:

Dave Bari
Helen Costello
Kathy Curotto
Nicki Dwyer
Mary Lois Engelbreit
Ginger Evans
Jean and Bob Fox
Pris Gontram
Virginia Hubbard
Jean Lowe
Lori Ann Malugen
Barbara Elliott Martin
Blair McNamee
Megan Miller
Isabelle and Jean-Paul Montupet
Harper Phillips
Stephanie Raaf
Elizabeth Richards
Joan Stevens
Delle Willet and the Missouri Botanical Gardens
Sonja Willman

When I was little, my sisters and I were constantly holding tea parties. There was always one going on somewhere around the house—in the yard, in our bedrooms. And even then we were into collecting, picking up tea sets at dime stores and garage sales.

The magic of tea is still very much alive for me, and the subject certainly has a way of popping up again and again in my illustrations. Admittedly, my work does chronicle and mirror my life, so you'll see plenty of tea parties among chil-

dren, dolls, and teddies (reminiscences of my own childhood) as well as tables set with tea things and cabinets displaying colorful pots and cups (reflections of how my home and my workplace look today).

I find the trappings of tea irresistible. And the idea of sitting down and taking tea with all the delicious trimmings is just so civilized and refreshing. You don't need to be English nobility to do it in style. You can do tea simply, with things you have on hand or great finds at flea markets and auctions. I always have my eye out for a lustreware sugar bowl and creamer or a fun set of dessert plates to perk up a tabletop. It's also fun to search boxes and bags of linens at swap meets and garage sales. You can never be sure that a cute tea cozy or set of placemats stitched with teacups and pots isn't waiting to be uncovered.

So won't you please join me and my crew of illustrated characters for this romp through the world of tea? I can promise some very fun ideas and inspiration. Just turn to any page.

Mary

chapter 1

Tea for You and Me

Tea is one of those simple luxuries—like a good bar of chocolate or a book—that truly enhances life with a minimum of fuss. You can make a ritual out of tea, enjoying a quiet cup in the morning by yourself, or one when you come home from work, or before you go to bed. "There is no companion so companionable as Solitude," Thoreau wrote. That's what tea represents for me: a moment of tranquility to reflect, being in my own company, of which I never tire. It's up to each of us to make life interesting. A moment spent with a cup of tea gives us time to plan and dream.

We really should count our blessings, you know. There was a time when tea was not available to everyone. Think about its origins: The Chinese had been enjoying it since the fourth century (at least!), and Europeans got their first tantalizing taste in the seventeenth century. Naturally, they were smitten and wanted some for themselves; since to get it required a long journey by ship, the prices were extremely high—the equivalent of thirty to fifty dollars per pound! No wonder tea-takers literally kept it under lock and key in their tea caddies.

Prices in the American colonies were just as exorbitant—if not more so. When those colonial rebels staged the Boston Tea Party on December 16, 1773, to protest a new tax by King George III, they precipitated the Revolutionary War. Clearly, tea lovers will go to great lengths to preserve their right to enjoy their favorite beverage.

So when you walk into a tea emporium and see the abundance on the shelves, don't forget to stop and smell the roses and jasmines, and the Lapsang souchong too.

Do not pass here

when you look for good tea.

Look, smell, and taste

as you wish,

but take some along.

—*sign in an eighteenth-century tea shop*

A Visit with the Camellias

When I first started reading about tea, I suddenly felt like I was back in school—and believe me, school wasn't the high point of my life. But then I realized that to enjoy tea, you don't have to become a connoisseur who can recite obscure statistics about which country each blend comes from. Rather, you just need to be able to enjoy the experience of sipping the tea. This section is, I hope, a gentle primer of tea terminology. Don't feel like you have to memorize the descriptions of each blend. Just keep them on hand for easy reference when planning future tea parties or choosing a blend just for you to enjoy.

There are so many kinds of tea—comprising over 3,000 varieties within the genus *Camellia*—that you might feel a little overwhelmed and automatically go for a familiar name. Why deprive yourself of the many possibilities when you could be savoring a great Darjeeling, an exquisite oolong, or a delicate green tea.

Yes, the terminology can be daunting: from first and second flush Darjeelings to impossible-to-pronounce Chinese types. And many beverages we call tea are not even members of the genus *Camellia*. Here's a primer that will soon have you talking tea.

Tea comes from an evergreen tree that is a member of the genus *Camellia*. The trees are kept to bush height, about three feet, but they could grow quite tall, to fifty feet or so. There's one in southwest China that's rumored to be eight hundred years old. The reason teas have so many different names not only has to do with how the leaves are fermented but also with the place where they're grown. Like wine, teas are named for a region or a special method of harvesting and processing them. Like a sommelier, an expert tea taster can tell where tea was grown and what time of year it was harvested. Did you know that women are considered the best tea leaf pluckers because their fingers are more nimble?

Black teas, the teas most commonly seen by Americans, are fully fermented. These lovely, full-bodied teas are perfect throughout the day, to perk you up in the morning and afternoon. They also waltz effortlessly into the evening (that is, if you don't mind the caffeine). Here are the basic varieties:

Darjeeling, often called the champagne of teas, is quite expensive. The ultimate is "first flush," picked in the spring in India's Himalayas. Darjeelings labeled flowery orange pekoe and golden flowery orange pekoe are made from leaves from the bud tips.

◎ ◎ ◎

Assam also comes from India. It is a robust tea, and the bigger the leaf, the better. It turns a rich mahogany with a splash of milk.

◎ ◎ ◎

Congou is a general term to describe all black teas from China.

◎ ◎ ◎

Keemun teas come from China and have a rich aroma. Since they fill the cup with their bright red liquor, these teas seem to lend themselves to festivity—and they take to milk.

Ceylon teas (from Sri Lanka) are grown in tea gardens high in the clouds. Perhaps that explains their magic: strong yet delicate, with hints of flowers.

Lapsang souchong is a mysterious Chinese tea with a smoky flavor produced by slow-firing over wood. Try it with cheese or spicy foods.

A friend of mine who grew up alongside a samovar has only one way to describe proper water for tea: "A mad boil."

—M.F.K. Fisher, "The Art of Eating"

Yunnan is like drinking liquid gold, which could explain why it has long been popular among Chinese nobility. This tea could also share the table with your breakfast muffins.

Nilgiri, from southern India, will put you in the mood for conversation. It's mellow, but still brisk.

Kenya black tea is strong and sweet: Add a touch of milk and you'll be savoring perfection. Try it first thing in the morning.

Bohea is one of the first cultivated varieties of the camellia plant; it turns a deep yellow color in the cup.

oolongs

You've doubtless had oolong tea before: It's served at Chinese restaurants. This partially fermented, brownish tea contains less caffeine than the black teas, but more than the greens. They are best drunk plain—no milk, sugar, or lemon.

Pouchong positively purrs with jasmine and gardenia. Also nutty tasting, it's nice on blustery winter days.

Black dragon is just a translation of "oolong," so the term refers to a broad variety of semifermented teas that have been dried over a charcoal fire. Among the black dragon group, Imperial oolong is prized for its honey flavor and appealing aroma. Lovely in the evening, Formosa oolong has a peachlike flavor. China oolong is less fermented, more delicate.

Ti Kuan Yin is a wonderful digestive.

Tung Ting swirls with pretty russet tones in the cup and is mild and lovely in the afternoon or evening. This tea looks just right steeping in a Chinese red clay teapot. A tea lover's tea.

When sorrows frown
What power can cheer
Or chase away the falling tear
Like Pekoe or Bohea.
What make the old
many young and strong
Like Hyson, Congou,
or Souchong.

—*Anonymous, "The Cup for Me"*

green teas

Completely unfermented, green teas are almost free of caffeine, so they are a nice option in the evening. Before World War II, Americans simply reveled in this tea, but after supplies were cut off, it became a largely forgotten pleasure. Until now.

Gunpowder is so named because the tea is rolled into little balls that explode, so to speak, upon contact with hot water. The tea has a yellowish-green tinge. Very nice in the afternoon. You'll find it in blends with mint.

Bancha tea is mild and refreshing. It helps you concentrate and think big thoughts.

Lung Ching helps clear the cobwebs from the brain—a wonderful tea for students and others who need to concentrate for long periods of time.

Hyson is a delicate green tea whose long, narrow, and twisted leaves are rolled into fine pearls or mixed with jasmine petals for jasmine tea. Young Hyson is plucked early.

Pi Lo Chun loosely translates to "spiral of Spring jade." If you're intrigued, seek out the finest tea dealer you can find, because this tea is relatively scarce and should be served at celebrations.

Silver dragon might sound ominous, but the name is really a reference to the appearance of the leaves, whose tinge and shape puts some in mind of a mythical beast. The tea is quite domesticated, thank you, and is light, sweet, and pleasantly scented.

classic blends

This is where everything you've learned comes together and where many of the fanciful names come from.

English Breakfast is a blend of black teas from Ceylon and India and goes quite nicely with milk. It's just right in the morning, naturally, and seems made for toast and jam—because it was.

Irish Breakfast is another strong blend of black teas (from Assam and Ceylon) and is good with milk and a lumberjack breakfast.

Earl Grey falls into the category of scented blends, because this (usually) black tea blend is flavored with oil of bergamot. It was named for the real Earl Grey, a nineteenth-century prime minister of England. A Chinese dignitary sent it to him in 1830 as a token of good faith and spawned a tea drinking tradition. It's nice with lemon and a platter of cakes. It's also lovely iced. (There are a number of other black tea blends that are named for famous people, but they are exclusive to the particular companies that develop them.)

Russian Caravan used to only be had after a long journey from China to Russia. Nowadays, this strong blend of blacks and oolongs is available to us. The Russians like to sip it through sugar cubes—take that as a hint to serve it iced, too.

Jasmine or Rose teas are proprietary Chinese blends in which blossoms impart their aroma to secret tea formulas. The blossoms are later removed, but you might find a few shyly peeking out. Fabulous with Asian cuisines.

Flavored teas are basically rich black teas containing spices or fruit essences—apricot, mango, passion fruit, gooseberry, boysenberry, lemon, and apple, to name a few of the many fruit flavors that are used.

Fruit Tea, Anyone?

Enhance hot tea by adding *chopped-up* pieces of *peeled* and *seeded* fruits to your teapot. Simply steep the fruit and tea together. It's fun to *pop in* peaches and pears or strawberries and kiwis. Another option is to *sprinkle* berry juice (pressed through a sieve) on tea leaves, allow them to dry, and then *brew* them up. This imparts a very subtle, refreshing taste to the teas.

herbal teas

Herbal teas are actually not teas at all. That is, they are herb mixtures made from roots, stems, and flowers—not from the leaves of tea plants. When you brew them into a "tea," you are making an infusion, what the French call a *tisane*. In France, *tilleul* is the most favored of herbal *tisanes*, a very pleasant infusion of linden tree leaves that's wonderful after dinner and seems to remedy whatever ails you. Chamomile runs a close second in popularity, with mint—perhaps blended with sweet marjoram and lemon verbena—being another favorite. They prefer their tea at five o'clock, and usually reserve a special pot for the brewing of *tisanes* alone. When it comes to herbs, the English prefer bee balm. After the Revolution, American colonists leaned toward strawberry and sweetbrier, or perhaps a sprig of lemon verbena sweetened with honey.

To properly infuse herbal tea, bring freshly drawn water to a boil, pour into a china or enamel teapot, and then sprinkle in the dried herb—one teaspoon per cup. Let steep five to ten minutes, covered, stirring occasionally. Strain into a cup, and perhaps sweeten it with honey.

It's easy to cultivate a few herbs on a window ledge to make fresh herbal teas year round. Some possibilities include angelica, basil, bay, lavender, lemon balm, lemon verbena, scented geraniums, and thyme. Choose a warm, dry spot, out of direct sun, to air-dry them in bundles, hanging from a rafter or wire. They could be dry in as little as two days, but usually a week is a safe bet.

TEA TIME

The tea bag was an accidental invention. Early in this century, American merchant Thomas Sullivan distributed samples of his tea in little silk packets. Customers liked the novelty and dipped the bags in hot water, rather than pouring out the contents into their tea strainers. The rest is history.

chapter 2

A Dress-up Party

"One of the luckiest things that can happen to you in life, I think, is to have a happy childhood," wrote Agatha Christie. I love that quote, because it really speaks to what's important for a child: a secure, nurturing environment supplemented by generous doses of fun and games. Nowadays, there are so many expensive, flashy toys with all the bells and whistles, but kids keep coming back to the old favorites, old-fashioned dolls and cuddly teddy bears—the same toys that I cherished when I was a child. I treated my toys to quite a few tea parties—nothing fancy, just fun. Parties like these—

and a loving family—went a long way toward counting me among the people whom Agatha Christie describes.

In many parts of England children still gather together for teatime in the midmorning and midafternoon, even in nursery school. As they sip their milky concoctions and feast on biscuits, cinnamon rolls, and jam cookies, they might be regaled with stories about tea or even rhymes. It was also during this "children's hour" that children whose lives were mostly spent with nannies got to spend time with their parents and feel ever-so-adult.

"You're going out for tea today,

Be careful what you do;

Let all accounts that I hear

Be pleasant ones of you."

—Kate Greenaway

The Tea Party

Why should British children have all the fun? American children adore tea (at least, the idea of tea) just as much, so why not throw a dress-up tea party at which girls and boys don costumes. The event can be as small or large as you please—whether a gathering of two best friends in a bedroom or a party of ten or more. It's even a nice way to celebrate a birthday.

The invitations could be cut out in the shape of teapots or cups; make a stencil from cardboard and just draw around it to repeat the pattern on paper. Or print the invitation on a doily, perhaps decorated with glued-on buttons, glitter, little candies, or even teapot stickers. These can be mailed in padded envelopes or hand-delivered on a Saturday morning by the child. Be sure to include the date, time (two or three o'clock is proper), and theme of the party, as well as your address and phone number.

Fill a chest or large basket with vintage clothing so that the children can dress themselves up, perhaps as a character from a favorite storybook, be it *Alice in Wonderland* or *Madeleine*. Thrift and consignment stores are a good source for showy clothes. Have lots of costume jewelry as well, the more glittery or dramatic, the better. And stock up on hats and fanciful scarves nabbed at garage sales and thrift shops.

Written in the Tea Leaves

When Alexander Pope wrote of "Matrons, who toss the cup and see/The grounds of fate in grounds of tea," he was referring, of course, to tea leaf readings, a popular pastime in the Scottish Highlands. It would certainly be a fun idea to hold a tea-leaf-themed Halloween party this year! Here's a quick guide so people will automatically assume you possess mysterious powers. First, brew up some loose tea in a pot. Pour the unstrained tea into each cup (use plain, unpatterned ones). Each person should drink up until almost the last sip, take the cup with two

Tell me gypsy, what can you see in my cup of tea?

hands and swirl in a clockwise direction, and then turn the cup over on

a saucer and allow the last of the tea to run off.

Now you're ready to read: Leaves in the bottom of the cup pertain

to the distant future; leaves at the top of the cup pertain to the near

future. Look for shapes made by the leaves: a horse means success, a

cow prosperity. Butterflies indicate attainment of happiness. Of course,

a ring means marriage and a heart is love. Trees mean good luck, while

anchors foretell of travel; ladders are symbols of success.

Can you predict my future, tell me my past?

—anonymous

When it comes to decorating, set the table as fancifully as you wish. Toys and figurines are charming accents. Child-size teacups are best for the tea, but don't be afraid to use inexpensive sets of your own. Children learn to be ever so careful while playing tea, and in their fine clothes, they'll try harder to be proper.

Do pepper the table with storybook references. Of course, it would be ideal to have a wonderful collectible like a forties Snow White teapot printed with the words "hi ho, hi ho." And if you head into any giftware store, you might come upon a new pot with a storybook theme. (You'd be surprised how quickly novelty pots like these appreciate in value over time.) But even a plain pot can be dressed for the occasion. For instance, an ordinary teapot could sport a homemade sign reading, "Drink Me," à la *Alice in Wonderland*.

"Take some more tea,"
the March Hare said to Alice very earnestly.
"I've had nothing yet,"
Alice replied in an offended tone:
"so I can't take more."
—Lewis Carroll, *Alice in Wonderland*

The tea itself could be any number of possibilities. Are you familiar with the term "cambric tea"? This is the kind served in English nurseries for centuries: simply a very milky tea with sugar to taste. Actually, the name comes from the French *thé de Cambrai,* named for tea whose color, with milk added, is reminiscent of the white Cambric linen fabric that originated in the city of Cambrai in France. The French use heavy cream and one full teaspoon of sugar per cup. If you want to make it very special, add a teeny bit of vanilla extract to each cup. Chamomile is another nice possibility, à la Beatrix Potter's *Peter Rabbit.* Some mothers dispense with tea altogether and serve watered-down white grape juice.

Cambric Tea Recipe:
hot water, milk, sugar and a small amount of tea.

"I can just imagine myself
sitting down at the head of the table
and pouring out the tea," said Anne,
shutting her eyes ecstatically.
"And asking Diana if she takes sugar!
I know she doesn't but
of course I'll ask her
just as if I didn't know."

—L.M. Montgomery, *Anne of Green Gables*

What to serve? Cupcakes are perfect (just be sure to call them teacakes). And even though it would be unheard of at a classic tea, it's perfectly fine to feature party favors like candy necklaces and gumdrops. But if you want a bit of tradition, consider serving bread and butter sandwiches shaped like hearts, diamonds, clubs, and spades, like the "pack of cards" in *Alice in Wonderland.* Cut off the crust from firm white and whole wheat loaves sliced thinly and use cookie cutters to make the shapes. Then butter the white breads and sandwich them together with a wheat bread. Keep chilled and covered in the refrigerator. Or serve cookies shaped like teapots and cups decorated with pastel icing. Be sure to cover them with plenty of icing squiggles, hearts, and flowers.

To keep the children from bouncing around too much, consider reading them a passage from a book that features tea. Or allow each child to read a passage from a different book. Excellent candidates are *Winnie the Pooh, Peter Pan, Anne of Green Gables,* and *The Wind in the Willows.* Send every child home with a teacup and saucer as a memento.

Recipe

Chocolate Dipped Strawberries

To make them, line a cookie sheet with waxed paper. Simmer water in a double boiler and add 12 ounces of bittersweet chocolate to the top. Or fill a heatproof bowl with the chocolate and butter and set in a saucepan of water. Stir with a wooden spoon until chocolate has melted, about 5 minutes. Pick up a strawberry by the leaves and dip into the chocolate, then place it on the waxed paper to set. Repeat with more strawberries—you should be able to use up a whole basket. Refrigerate until ready to serve.

Little ones love to be mother's helpers when it comes to making cookies. There are plenty of ways to put their hands to use: If the child is old enough, let him or her roll out the dough or even measure and mix the ingredients. But if the junior cookie chef is very young, simpler tasks like adding sprinkles are best. For children who love to draw and color, making teapot and teacup cookies is a fun way to spend the afternoon. Use professional food coloring to tint the icing—so much prettier than the kinds sold at the super-market. You'll find the professional kinds at bakers' supply and crafts stores. And make sure your pastry bag has plenty of different-size tips so you can vary the designs (we used Mary Engelbreit tea-themed stickers for inspiration). Also, look for cookie cutters shaped like teacups and pots—if none turn up, just cut the shapes from a cardboard template you make yourself.

The Nursery Tea

On a rainy day when housebound children complain that there's nothing to do, throw a tea party in the nursery, where dolls and teddies pull up a chair.

First things first: Word needs to be spread around the nursery, just so everyone knows. One scrolled invitation, perhaps tied with a ribbon and unfurled and read aloud in a booming voice would do nicely:

"Nursery tea today—two o'clock sharp. All dolls, stuffed animals, toys, and pets invited."

One clever little girl actually converted an old potting shed in her backyard into a "tearoom" called The Morning Glory Cafe, where she serves an ongoing round of Raggedy Anns and Andys, stuffed bears, plastic dinosaurs, and a trio of cats (they take their tea with milk, and hold the tea). She recommends writing up

a menu and setting it on a play table (frame it if the occasion is formal).

Nursery tea today—
two o'clock sharp.
All dolls, stuffed animals, toys
and pets invited.

"Cambric tea was hot water and milk,

with only a taste of tea in it,

but little girls felt grown-up

when their mothers let them drink

Cambric tea."

—Laura Ingalls Wilder, *The Long Winter*

THE TOYS' TEA PA

The dolls and animals will have to be dressed up, naturally. So get out the play combs and ribbons and start grooming them for the occasion, perhaps with new sashes at the dolls' waists, or new hairstyles. The stuffed animals might look sharp in vintage hats and cravats. Pets tend to resist dressing up properly, though a bit of catnip or a dog biscuit seems to help things along.

Dolls and stuffed animals tend to be a tight-lipped crowd, but did you know that one of their absolutely favorite all-time teatime treats is brown bread and butter with a little honey (especially for the stuffed bears)? Oh, yes, and the sugar sandwiches! Spread thin white bread with butter and sprinkle on some sugar. Mashed up bananas on toast are another favorite. Or if your child likes fairies and elves, simply use leaves as "saucers" and acorn tops as "cups," just like they do in the land of make-believe.

"Your Aunt D'Aubert instructed me
to give you this little tea set as a gift from her."
. . . The delighted Sophie took the tray
with its six cups, teapot, silver sugar bowl, and creamer.

—Comtesse d'Ségur, *Les Malheurs de Sophie*

There can also be a make-believe tea taking place in the dollhouse. If you have doll-size tea sets, by all means put those to use. Some are actually made of translucent china and can really pour pretend tea for the dolls. A word to the wise: Dolls hardly ever notice if their "tea" is actually sugar water.

Tiny Teasets

If you walk into any large antiques store, you're bound to come across any number of small tea sets. Once you open your eyes to them, you'll discover the tiny pots and plates all around—peeking out of display cases, nestling among antique dolls on shelves. Small tea sets are wonderful to collect because they take up much less room than their full-size counterparts, though some can be even pricier.

There are really four types of tiny tea sets: children's, individual, toy, and doll (including miniatures). To distinguish between them, use the information here as a general guide.

If a teapot can pour two or more small servings and the cup can hold three to four ounces, you're in possession of a children's set. These were originally made for children to really use, and some of the finest examples date from the nineteenth century and the Edwardian period, when English children in wealthy families often had their own quarters and mingled very little with adults; therefore, they needed their own child-sized dishes.

If the teapot holds one cup (as opposed to six for a standard pot), the set is an individual size, made as souvenirs, novelties, and commemoration. For instance, a typical miniature set includes a pot, plate, and cup and comes with its own miniature display rack.

Anything smaller than what we've

COME LITTLE
COTTAGE GIRL,
YOU SEEM TO
WANT a CUP of TEA;

AND WILL YOU TAKE
a LITTLE CREAM?
NOW TELL the
TRUTH TO ME.

· BARRY PAIN ·

just discussed falls into the category of toy or doll size, which also includes minia-

ture teapots and tea sets (also intended for display). Toy tea sets are just what the

name implies—toys—and are meant for play with brothers, sisters, or friends

(though dolls and teddies can use them too). These often include

painted scenes, figures, or other decals or designs. The last cate-

gory—doll sized—which may include miniature teapots and

tea sets, is simply for display or pretend with dolls and in doll-

houses. Too small even for child-size hands, these sets are particu-

larly intriguing because of their tiny forms. These miniatures may have intrigu-

ing little details, like pink little flowers and gold trim. And some are made of

translucent china—for don't dolls deserve a bit of luxury too?

chapter 3

Out with Friends

Have you ever noticed that there's never a "perfect" moment for getting together with friends? Everyone's so busy, running to the gym, carpooling, grocery shopping—not to mention earning a living. How can you take time to socialize when you can barely keep up with the laundry? Simple: Just make a date. When you make time, there is time. Even if I have some looming deadline for a set amount of greeting cards, I still meet with my friends on a regular basis. You know that old saying, "Work expands or contracts to fill the amount of time you have to do it?" It's true. I find that the amount of

63

time spent with friends rewards me over and over: I return to my drawing board with plenty of inspiration, which means that half my work is already done! A tea party at a hotel or tearoom is a great way to socialize because then there's no burden on any one person to "entertain."

It feels so good to have a *friend*
on whom you can depend.
A *friend* can help to mend a heart,
boost you toward a brand-new start,
clown with carefree, schoolgirl glee,
share a quiet cup of tea.

—Jan Miller Girando, *Pals*

T·I·M·E for T·E·A

Usually we are all too busy to stop and do something for ourselves, so taking time out for tea is a lovely change of scenery. It's also a way for friends to get together and catch up. So why not invite some friends to tea? A handwritten invitation on elegant notecards would be just fine. Just say when and where, with your number for regrets only. Everyone is sure to come—so make your reservation with the tearoom. Three seatings are fairly common, falling somewhere around 1:00 P.M., 2:30 P.M., and 4:00 P.M.—do check.

It keeps the eye wakeful, the head clear, animates the intellectual powers.

—Thomas Short, *Discourse on Tea*

High, Low, and Cream Teas

Afternoon tea as we know it was not invented so very long ago. The story goes that in 1840, Anna, the seventh duchess of Bedford, was waiting around with other noblewoman types for their husbands to return from the hunt so that they could dine. By late afternoon, they were getting quite famished, and so the duchess ordered cakes and sandwiches to be served in her boudoir.

The ritual moved to the drawing room and became a time of social calls. But it was called low tea, not high. Cream tea is a reference to the presence of cream as part of the menu, for instance, strawberries and scones with Jersey cream. Elevenses is the name for the morning tea or coffee break in Britain.

High tea is actually the working man's light supper of lunchtime leftovers. You might wish to serve this as a buffet, with hot dishes, pies, and cold, hearty sandwiches at the ready. Also have a bit of cake. And don't worry about niceties: Serve the tea in large steaming mugs, rather than in low tea's dainty porcelain cups.

■ ■ ■ ■ ■

As you enter the door, you're greeted by sweet and pungent aromas, you seem to drift across time. And you'll suddenly remember why you're here, even if you had to rush and were secretly thinking about the millions of things you "should" be doing: One of life's greatest pleasures, along with hot baths and watching sunsets, is a proper cup of tea.

Soft music will undoubtedly be playing. If you are in luck, there might even be a trio—the kind that used to serenade tea dancers as they whirled around the room in times past. Or maybe someone's tinkling away on the baby grand. And if it is an English-style tearoom, it might boast all that amiable clutter that makes them so inviting, down to the china jugs on the shelves and portraits on the wall. In really homey places, the tea could even be served in a crocheted tea cozy, while in more elegant urban tea rooms, the tea might be rolled up on a mahogany cart and served in individual pots, with boiling water drawn from a silver samovar. Honey crumpets, scones with Jersey cream and berries, and finger sandwiches followed by small cakes or tea loaves are the norm.

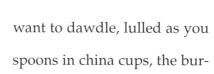

You'll undoubtedly want to dawdle, lulled as you are by the clink of silver spoons in china cups, the burble of boiling water, and naturally the conversation among friends. No surreptitious glances at your wristwatch allowed.

Maybe there is no tearoom in your general vicinity. Not to worry. Host your own afternoon tea. Offering tea is simply an extension of friendship, so if it seems less daunting, think of this as a "friendship tea."

Setting the table is easy enough. You'll need a tray—any tray—so long as it's large enough to hold a teapot, a pot of hot water for diluting the tea, a pitcher of milk, a bowl of sugar cubes or other sweetener, and two little plates: one for lemon slices and another for holding the tea strainer. If you like, cover the tray with a fun cloth: checks, floral, polka dots—whatever looks nice with your tea things. Place your cups and saucers on the table to the left of the tea tray (or the right if you're left handed). Add a teaspoon to each saucer. Stack the tea and dessert plates, forks and napkins nearby.

The menu can be as simple as you please. Plan on two types of tea sandwiches, a little plate of cute tea cookies, and one great dessert, whether a fruit tart or a cream cake. For the teas, go with a traditional afternoon type, like Darjeeling or orange pekoe blends.

First add the milk and sugar or the lemon to the teacup. Now pour in the tea, leaving space for the addition of hot water if the guest prefers a weaker tea. Next pass the dessert plates, napkins, and forks, then the sandwiches, followed by cookies and, finally, the tea dessert.

Recipes

Tea Sandwiches

Here are some sandwich possibilities: pecan-studded cream cheese with chive butter; almond chicken with basil butter; cucumber with creamed butter; avocado slices with Dijon dressing; curried egg salad; rare roast beef on lightly buttered bread; watercress and thinly sliced tomatoes. Use good quality wheat, pumpernickel, date nut, and white breads, all with crusts trimmed, naturally, and cut into four small triangular sandwiches. Plan on eight sandwiches per person.

Fancy Butters

To make flavored butters for tea sandwiches and scones, just mix together one cup of unsalted, softened butter with the ingredients of choice in an electric mixer. Then spoon it into a pretty serving bowl. Some possibilities for the butter include an herb butter of parsley, tarragon, thyme, and white pepper. This is wonderful with smoked salmon or asparagus.

Or make a dainty flower butter. Mix edible, organically grown flower petals--such as roses, violets, calendula, and borage--with butter in a bowl. Then cover a flat surface with plastic wrap. Place the butter on the wrap and roll into a small log shape using the plastic wrap. Press petals around the outside of the log, wrap tightly, and chill until ready to use.

chapter 4

A Wedding Tea

ust like most any artist, I went through my lean years, and I know all about living on a budget. I've found that you don't need a whole lot of money to be happy. Just lighting candles at the dinner table and adding a bouquet of wildflowers can make all the difference. So when it comes to hosting a party—in this case, a tea honoring the bridal party—don't think that you have to spend tons of money. Rather, work with what you've got. Bring out your most beautiful china (or borrow some), snip flowers from the backyard, brew up the tea, and enlist friends to help you with the foods.

a wedding tea

Remember, imaginative presentations of fresh vegetables, sandwiches, cookies, and other inexpensive foods can delight the eye (and palate) without breaking the budget. For instance, crudité on a pink, lacy-edged platter looks far more appealing than on plain white dishes.

Here's a tea that the mother of the bride can host, inviting all her bridesmaids. This could also be the occasion of a shower. Or if it's a small, at-home wedding, you could simply expand on this idea for the reception.

The tea-table offered
an anomalous
and picturesque repast;
and on leaving it
they all sat and talked
in the large piazza,
or wandered about
the garden
in the starlight.

—Henry James, The Europeans

Irish tea linens, three-tiered and plates of divine sandwiches, a are the ingredients for this opulent silver caddies bearing petit fours canopy dancing in the wind . . . such occasion. You needn't go into lifelong debt. Just get out grandmother's china and any pretty silver things you have and borrow the rest.

The centerpiece of the buffet table should be something fun and fresh, maybe a framed photo of the bridal couple, edged in dried baby roses. Garland the table with whatever fresh flowers you like: peonies, roses, even a chain of wildflowers. All-white themes could include roses and lillies of the valley or gardenias. Or swag the sides with fresh fragrant greens, like artemisia, held in place by satiny white ribbons. It's especially fun to fill the table with retro cake toppers, so brides and grooms from decades past can join the festivities.

For this event, you'll want to dress up the sandwiches to the hilt. Make three-tiered types, alternating white and wheat breads. Consider a more exotic turn, perhaps rolled-up pinwheels of dark pumpernickel with papaya cream

cheese swirling around a platter; half moons of whole wheat bread plumped up with slivers of chilled prime rib roast and sealed with horseradish cream cheese; or a sandwich with rippling ribbons of dilled cream cheese and smoked salmon. The natural, jewel-like tones of a fresh fruit salad are also a nice touch.

The true art of giving a wedding breakfast
is to introduce as much variety
in the menu as possible,
and to tempt the appetite
with light and
appétisant delicacies.

—Anonymous, "Party-Giving on Every Scale"

If you like, add scones with jams, softened butter, and clotted cream. Serve the scones on footed platters and the butter, jams, and creams in cut glass jars that will glimmer in the sun. For dessert, a simple pound cake served with fresh berries or berry tarts are divine. Or dress up cakes with ivory icing.

The tea should be something celebratory. Use a samovar for hot water, or press your automatic coffee maker into service; just use a little extra loose tea because it won't be steeping for as long a period of time as in the pot. Coffee presses are also good: Add the tea, boiling water, and steep. Trap loose tea under the plunger before serving. Or create a concentrate by using a quart of water poured over two-thirds of a cup of leaves. Steep and strain into a teapot or pitcher. Now the concentrate is ready when you are. If you do go with tea bags, figure on one tea bag for every two people; for instance 44 people would require 22 bags and about two gallons of water.

Whatever you do, offer a selection of fine teas—such as Lapsang souchong, Earl Grey, and Russian Caravan—with sugar cubes, lemon slices with cloves

A Special Occasion Punch

For a very special punch, use brewed black tea as a base—it imparts a delicious background flavor. Orange juice, citrus slices, and mint leaves are also nice additions. The punchbowl can decorate the table if you garland it in a ring of flowers or tie on a satiny ribbon.

If you're going to add soda, champagne, or sparkling wine to your punch, serve it at the last minute to retain the bubbles. And remember to pour it down the sides of the bowl.

You might also want to use decorative ice cubes: Fill the ice tray one-third full with water and freeze until it is partially frozen. Add tiny garnishes like edible flowers, mint sprigs, or currants; refreeze. Then add a sealing layer of water and freeze the cubes completely.

studded in the rinds, and fresh milk. Consider also serving an iced tea.
If you do, keep refreshing the drink with tea
ice cubes—they're made from double-
strength tea and frozen, with sugar.
And because it's a special occasion,
fortify the table with sherry or
champagne in silvery buckets.
Cheers!

chapter 5

Tea Indoors and Out

Whenever someone asks me where I get my best ideas, I always reply, "Shopping." And I'm serious, because going to flea markets, auctions, and antiques stores really inspires me. Seeing a pattern on a piece of china or a vintage toy can give me enough inspiration for a month of work. I like being alone, but shopping with friends is the ultimate. I regularly get together with a group of women who call ourselves "the fleabags." Each one of us is hunting down a special thing and it's fun to not only be on the lookout for your own collectibles but for your friends' as well.

Collecting

When pressed, I'd probably admit that my real love of tea has to do with all the accoutrements. For me, tea is an excuse to bring them out and use them—though I always have them on display anyway. I still have many of the tea sets I played with as a girl (that is, the ones that didn't get broken), and considering that I started going to antique stores and flea markets with my mother when I was small, I have managed to build up quite a collection of child- and adult-size tea things.

Lustreware is one of my all-time favorites, in particular the art deco kind that's glazed with a metallic film to give it a shimmering quality. These pieces have such whimsy about them, whether they're topped by sculptural birds or

decorated with scenes of abstract flowers and elegant women. I've acquired quite a few creamers and sugars, and I display them on my living room shelves; in fact, their sprightly, iridescent colors actually inspired the color scheme for the entire room. You won't have trouble spotting them when you're out flea-marketing in

the early morning: It's easy to pick their shimmering shapes right out of a crowd of collectibles. The really fun stuff was produced by the Japanese company Noritake, starting in the '20s and continuing through the '40s. Look for the Noritake name, the words "Nippon" or "Japan," or an "M" garlanded in leaves.

Tea time is also an opportunity to bring out my cute collection of sterling silver teaspoons with the name of the state or city on the handle. My grandfather would bring them to my grandmother from his business trips, and I'm the lucky recipient of the entire lot (I'll admit they're not quite as highbrow as sterling silver Victorian caddy spoons that are also very popular collectibles, but they're a lot more fun). When they're not in use, they look great grouped in a clear glass.

For me, teapots are much more than mere vessels to hold the beverage. They're conversation pieces and they can be the starting point for a party. If you want to collect, there will certainly be competition, because there is a thriving community of aficionados, some of whom specialize in particular eras or themes.

Enter their world and you'll find smiling apple-face teapots from 1950s Japan and psychedelic-looking owls made in the same country a decade later. Then there are the '40s-era British Indian tepee teapots (the handle has a totem pole face and the tea pours from a chieftain's headdress) and perky pink pigs from postwar Germany. You're sure to come across those adorable English thatched-roof cottage teapots from the '30s and '40s (many made in Japan, but some also in England). America has also turned out some classics, like Oklahoma-made '40s teapots shaped like wagonwheels or the famous red-donut teapots and cobalt-blue twinspouts produced by Hall China of Ohio in the '30s and '40s.

Don't forget about the pottery kind; one thing you'll commonly see if you live in the northern states are chocolate-brown Canadian teapots with tulips and leaves painted over the glaze.

Another fun collectible is the curious majolica-style teapots made in Japan. If you're lucky, you might find a set with teapot, salt and peppers, cream and sugar, toothpick holder, and vase, all with the same motif. This would typically have been sold at dimestores like F.W. Woolworth's or S.S. Kresge's. Their colors were typically earthy and splashed on, and they usually have some kind of background motif—like a basketweave—along with a primary decoration. Examples include an absurd yet appealing octagonal pot with a scratch-weave background and a depiction of a blue elephant grazing among green and yellow daisies.

Displaying and Decor

When it comes to displaying your tea collectibles, don't hesitate to group many different eras of teasets together. I see no reason to confine them to cabinets. Let tea pots march along shelves, sit on coffee tables (perhaps sprigged with a bouquet of fresh flowers), and hold your desktop pens and pencils. Some people have found that teapots also make good knitting companions. Just put the wool in the pot and pull it out through the spout. And it's not unheard of to convert a teapot into a lampbase—especially charming for lighting a reading nook where you settle in with a cup of tea daily.

*When teapots of different eras, shapes,
and sizes come together,
the result is always delightful.*

Even if there's no room for a floor-to-ceiling
display case, a Victorian-style wall-hung
whatnot does the job nicely.

Majolica tea sets shaped like vegetables and fruits are functional sculptures that you never need to put away.

Tea sets are so irresistible, they have inspired a whole slew of motifs to decorate the world at large. For instance, old blown-glass Christmas tree ornaments were sometimes made to resemble tea sets, and who can forget those wonderful amusement park cups-and-saucers rides? If you're lucky, you might even come across an old plastic shade-pull in the shape of a teacup, popular in the '50s. You can revive that idea by dangling miniature cups by their handles from curtain rods in a child's room. We've also found teacups on furniture, used as motifs for the drawer pulls of a jelly cupboard.

° ° °

I'm writing this in bed. Living here is very luxurious, my breakfast tray set with the most beautiful Limoges china....

—Oswald Wynd,
The Ginger Tree

Tea for One

To be perfectly realistic, it's the rare person who has an hour to spend each afternoon preparing and enjoying tea. Instead, try to catch a few minutes for yourself—maybe when you come home from work, the perfect time to declutter your mind. Just set aside a corner with a tin or bags of your favorite tea, a box of biscuits or cookies, your cup, and an individual teapot. Keep them in the same place, so you'll always be ready to take tea.

Another option is to grab a mug of tea with a few biscuits around three o'clock at the office. If there's a conference room, invite your coworkers to share tea with you. You'll all feel more relaxed—and you'll be more productive when you return to work.

You could also make tea-taking a bedtime ritual (decaf, of course). Chamomile is a favorite choice, but rosehips, mint, or a fresh spray of lemon verbena with a touch of honey will do nicely.

And don't forget that tea for one is a lovely way to surprise someone you love. On Mother's Day, for instance, you might put together a lovely tray of morning tea, with a selection of toast and jam.

Tea Themes

Don't let the tea themes we've presented thus far limit you! These are truly the tip of the iceberg. There are all sorts of other tea celebrations you can indulge in, too. For instance, initiate a family tradition of tea every Sunday afternoon. There's this fabulous novel by Carol Shields called *Small Ceremonies* in which a family that spent a year living in England brings that custom with them back to their home in Canada to enjoy on Sunday afternoons. Or consider making tea the beverage of choice at your next brunch. Institute your own "fireside chats" with your spouse with a soothing pot of tea between you. Or bring along a thermos of tea on a hike in the woods to enjoy autumn foliage. I'll bet you can think of a zillion more ideas.

Just like a professional wine tasting, the "cupping" of tea is how tea is evaluated. And just as with the fruit of the vine, there is a great deal of terminology associated with tea grading. "Toasty" refers to aroma; "winy" to the mellowness; "brisk" to the "live" quality of the tea. You can invite over friends and hold your own tea tasting and use any terminology you wish—and at the same time you'll be able to put your teapot collection to use. Simply infuse six pots of tea with different types—but don't tell anyone what they are. Keep track of which teas are in which pots. Then bring out the tea tins or bags and have your friends

match them up. It's a way to learn about different types of tea and savor the subtleties.

In the Garden

When you take iced tea outdoors, you have an opportunity to accessorize in an entirely new way. Rather than teacups, decorative glassware—such as candy-stripe Murano glass—has a way of making a table instantly glitter. And pick up some clear-stemmed or colored-glass Italian swizzle sticks, perhaps topped by stripes or little balls. They glint like ribbon candy in the sun and look adorable clustered in a little vase on the table. Don't forget about silver iced tea sippers, which are silver straws with little spoons at the end. You can buy them by the half dozen at flea markets. Of course, this is also a chance to use your most gorgeous glass pitchers, accessorized with sprigs of mint and bobbing slices of oranges and lemons.

Recipes

Sun Tea

You'll need the morning for this one.
In a one gallon jar with a lid, add
three quarts cold water to six table-
spoons of loose tea or six tea bags.
Add the lid and place the jar in a
sunny window or outdoors directly
in the sun for three hours. Strain,
add whatever ingredients you
wish—1/4 cup of sugar or honey, a
few mint sprigs, a sliced lemon—
and chill. (If you're taking it on an
outing, remove the lemon and mint
and pour in a thermos.) Another
way to steep the tea is simply to let
it sit in the refrigerator overnight.
Cold-water-brewed teas tend not to
cloud.

Iced Tea

Follow all the directions given earlier for making hot tea (boil water, steep three to five minutes), except double the amount of tea used per cup: two teaspoons of loose tea or one tea bag per cup. After it has steeped, remove bags or strain tea into a pitcher three-fourths full with ice. Then add your favorite accompaniments: sugar, lemon, or mint sprigs.

Here in St. Louis we are particularly fond of iced tea, and with good reason. It seems there was a terrible heat wave in 1904 at the St. Louis World's Fair Louisiana Purchase Exhibition. An Indian exhibitor had a brainstorm for flagging sales of hot tea: Simply pour it over ice. As the ice cubes clinked, the idea clicked.

Here are some intriguing possibilities for ice-cold thirst quenchers:

- Darjeeling spiced with five cloves and juice of one whole orange and lime
- lemon and mint teas garnished with fresh mint
- strawberry tea with sugar and lemon

When you take tea outdoors, that doesn't necessarily mean that everyone must gather around a lace-covered table, Jane Austen style. I've seen vintage photos of tea takers lying on deck chairs on cruise ships as well as bathing beauties sitting poolside with flowered caps on their heads and steaming cups in their hands. (Whether or not it's an old wives' tale, it's said that a cup of hot tea on a hot day actually cools you off—maybe it's because the steaming temperature of the tea makes everything else seem chilly in comparison.)

Just like coffee lovers who wouldn't consider traveling without beans, a grinder, and filters, there are confirmed tea drinkers who always pack kettles, pots, and mugs when they're on the road. And they're not just English. The French have long considered tea to be an essential part of the art de vivre. Since the nineteenth century, they've produced wicker baskets complete with full tea services to enjoy this beverage anywhere. Why not adopt this line of thinking and introduce tea to your next tailgate party? Or, to borrow a scene from my life, tote along hot or cold tea to share with friends and refresh your senses after a morning of garage sales.

They sat down to tea—
the same party round the same table—
how often it had been collected!
—and how often had her eyes fallen
on the same shrubs in the lawn,
and observed the same beautiful effect
of the western sun!

—*Jane Austen, Emma*

A Sporting Tea

In the early 1900s, the great lawns of private estates were filled with countless croquet and badminton fanatics. They spent their summers "sending," "smashing," and "splitting each other" until dinnertime. Naturally, all this running about required some kind of continual refreshment, and so tea was often served on the lawn and courtside, amid the badminton shuttlecocks and rosewood mallets. Should you do the same, consider enjoying it iced, served with a plate of fruit.

A Dance in the Garden

During the eighteenth century, tea gardens were the place to be in London. Vauxhall, Ranalagh, Cuper's Garden, and Marylebone were the most renowned, and though they were patronized by royalty, everyone was free to go there for a stroll and a cup of tea—along with other refreshments. As if this weren't enough, during the late afternoon into the evening, there were concerts in the arbors with bands set up under gazebos and couples gliding arm in arm under the boughs. The custom popped up again in the Hotel Palm Courts of the Victorian era, and some tearooms today are reviving this very lovely way of taking tea.

By now I hope you'll agree with me that tea is just about the most fun thing on earth. I know that I've learned a lot about this drink, and I no longer think that you have to be British to truly savor it. I've made a lot of new resolutions about how I'm going to take time out to enjoy it with my friends and family.

And now that I'm a full-throttle tea drinker, I have even more of an excuse to shop for pots, cups, saucers, spoons, and strainers than ever before. Finger sandwiches, anyone?

The end.

credits

American Doodah/Joan Stevens, Webster Groves, Missouri
vintage linens

Christopher's Home Accents, Kirkwood, Missouri
wire teapot

Cornucopia, St. Louis, Missouri
tea package location

Davis Place Antiques, Clayton, Missouri
bride and groom cake toppers

Legacy Antiques, Clayton, Missouri
teacup collection, tea packages, and jars of tea

Sonja Willman Design, St. Louis, Missouri
bedroom tea